—

Visions in Rhyme

Sabrina Willmer

BROWN
DOG
BOOKS

Published under licence by Brown Dog Books and
The Self-Publishing Partnership Ltd, 10b Greenway Farm, Bath Rd,
Wick, nr. Bath BS30 5RL

www.selfpublishingpartnership.co.uk

ISBN printed book: 978-1-83952-375-5
ISBN e-book: 978-1-83952-376-2

Cover design by Kevin Rylands
Internal design by Andrew Easton

Printed and bound in the UK

This book is printed on FSC certified paper

I dedicate my book to my kids Saur, Frank, Kimberley, Melanie, Luke, and Antonia; and my grand-kids Maya, Joshua, Crimson, Erin, Abigail, Annabel, and Alice and my best friend Kuli.

Also to my Nana Muriel, Dada Jack and my little brother Cornel: gone but not forgotten... x

With special thanks to Victor Jackson.

Introduction

When on the way to finding the truth don't let anything stop you. For only when you truly know the answers to all will you find inner peace. The hold-ups and the hang-ups that halt and restrict are there as teachers, as keys to locked doors. So use them as aids to make your journey easier; rather than seeing them as handicaps or as barriers. Everything in your life has a purpose, everyone has a reason for being there. See their intention, understand their presence. 'No one can stop you.' 'Nothing is in the way.' If these two affirmations can be used as positive levers in your life much can be accomplished.

Sometimes life throws at us, a great deal more than we can handle, sometimes unfair things are done to us. At times like these, anger, resentment, frustration, and all of these negative emotions surge forward, like an army trying to knock us out of the picture. But for every negative emotion within, there is a positive one ready to heal the pain. Only you can realise it into being. If you are angry then let forgiveness take its place. If you are frustrated learn patience. If you resent then learn to love. It is easy to love when you are loved and appreciated, but not so easy when you send out and do all the right things, and still you are left out in the cold. But if you are strong and realise your positive qualities into existence, when things are unfair and tiresome, you truly are on the right path the joy and happiness and all that you give out will surely return to you.

It is simple to know the truth, but the hardest part is living that truth. How many times have we known what is needed of us yet, did just the opposite? Maybe it was easier or we were tempted due to our own weaknesses. But because it was not the right thing to do, we usually had to suffer the consequences and the discomfort felt from the lesson being taught. Now if we had done the right thing from the start, the strong gut feeling we get when we are being shown the right way, 'OUR INTUITION' the lesson would not have been necessary. As if we had trusted our own instinct we would have saved ourselves a whole lot of time and trouble. Most of us take the easy way out, or we usually trust what we can see more than what we can feel – and that's where we go wrong. Our eyes deceive us, our ears could hear things that could mislead us, our smell can wrongly arouse us, our minds can play tricks on us with contradictory thoughts. But, if we shut our eyes, plugged our ears and nose, if we switched off our minds for just a few moments, what's left? Our invisible sense; this is the greatest gift of all.

We should learn to sharpen this invisible aid we have. How many times have you got things spot on just by that sense, it's 100% right, but most of us don't use the greatest gift we have. It is dulled by our weakness of not trusting. God has given us this gift; this ability, so that we can avoid the pitfalls and the many dead ends we fall trap to. It is up to us to use this ability and to use it all the time. The enormous benefits from the sharpening up of the sixth sense will become apparent when you start to trust your instinct and do what you believe is right.

Once you realise you can always make the right choices and decisions in your life, that you can avoid danger, that you can always be sure of all that you are doing, the negative emotions, doubt and fear need never hold you back again. Being unsure is very time consuming and tiring, we make mistakes, we take what's being offered because we haven't a clue of what we want. When we doubt we are sure to lose, or end up with something we don't want. We restrict ourselves to a vicious circle where doubt and fear exist and rules our lives. Doubt and fear will hinder progress and delay success. Doubt and fear are the enemy, listen within and be what you want to be. It's true you can be whatever you want to be. Everyone is a potential leader. We can all be leaders in our own right, if we can pass on whatever we learn to others who are still searching. We are, in a manner, leading them out of their dark hours through life's lessons learnt. That is why I said earlier everything and everyone is our teacher, including one's self.

My way of putting something back is in my poems. I've tried to keep them short and sweet. Each one has a special message for you. Close your eyes, relax and open a page, read a poem for that day, or maybe when you're feeling uncertain or unhappy choose a number and that poem can uplift and help you see your way through. These poems are gentle yet powerful in their meaning and I hope that by reading them you too can start to express yourself with a clearer understanding.

Go with God

'Sabrina'

Myself

As a child, I was so sad,
The memories don't always make me glad.
My mother did leave me, oh so long ago,
My father did abuse me, all the while I did grow.
Instead of love, instead of care, beatings and
rapings. It just wasn't fair.
Many a time, I mistook sex for love,
my mind confused, I prayed to him above.
In time, I met a man who did love me.
I bore his children, and thought I was free.
To enjoy this life in love and care but once
again, life turned unfair.
Out of the blue, God took him away.
He died, my love, one summer's day.
My children and I, Oh, did we cry!
Life seemed to throw at us blow after blow
I stopped one day and asked God why?
He told me my tears to dry.
I listened to what he had to say
The silent voice within said, Hey!
Do you know how special you are?
In my eyes you truly are a star.
I do know now, that I must live,
My life in service of others, to give,
Whatever is needed through word or by touch,
Nobody's problem will ever be too much.
My faith in God has pulled me through,
I await in patience
His work to do.

'Sabrina'

1.

God's children are we, never a doubt,
when life takes a tumble, and there's
no one about.
Look up and see
He is smiling
Loving you, guiding you
Making a way for your salvation
A bright beautiful day.

2.

Man alone cannot find the answers to
all he is so blind.
They are beside him always awaiting
God's angels never tiring, never failing,
Together to find mysteries unfolding
Trusting and giving whatever is needed
Together to win if voices are heeded.

3.

The hunger pangs that you receive,
to learn more about life can sometimes deceive.
Your thirst for knowledge starts to weaken,
when your ego, starts to beckon.
There are no ways or methods proven,
to get closer to the truth unwoven.
But if you keep that light inside burning,
you will soon start to do some learning.

4.

When darkness enfolds your very being,
Take time out and call Him to your side.
Allow Him to heal you, a little at a time.
The hard times may test your love to extremes,
And sometimes we give up but never does He.
Place your trust in Him beyond,
And travel to this path no time to waste.
Learning can be so much fun,
With humour around your work's soon done.

5.

A word can caress, or sting with pain
If harsh words are spoken nothing remains
A kind word here,
A kind word there.
Bring about healing, creating love to spare.
Use your words wisely and soon you will see,
People around you smiling at thee.

6.

On the path of truth
There is only gain.
The stuff you lose
Is excess and vain.
Giving up is getting tenfold,
A bargain if ever,
Hey I'm sold.
So let go and see
A miracle unravel,
Making your journey easier to travel.

7.

Be your own witness and make a stand.
Shout loud and clear your message so grand.
Given to you by special angels sent down.
To make life easier when there's a frown.
So each of you, now know without each other
very little grows.
Come along now and banter with me,
For in God's eternal plan
we all will be free.

8.

Chase away the shadows
That darken up your day.
They have no power in your life
If you call out and pray.
They are only a distraction,
A moment maybe more.
If you are quick enough to shut that
beastly door.
Help is always there, if you need it.
So don't be afraid, grab out and use it.
For if in your heart you have the right
reasons.
God will protect you
Through all seasons.

9.

Give thanks always
For what you've been 'given'
No matter how big or small
While in this life, you're 'livin''
Returning the favour to origin.
For if you are always on the take
and not appreciating what you make.
Alone, you may find yourself one day.
For have you not heard them say
'As you sow, so shall you reap'
In your heart, do this keep.

10.

Listen to the voice that's calling,
It calls out to you to set the ball rolling.
So little time is left you see
To make amends to free.
All God's creatures big and small
From man's self-destruction
we're heading for a fall.
So do your bit, until everything fits
Back into God's plan.

11.

A smile, can change so much you know
Your face beams, your heart does glow
Sometimes it could be a cheeky grin,
A tough situation, you could win,
By just a smile, someone you could cheer
A warm feeling descends on someone
who's dear.
A frown your forehead cannot crease
When a smile beams at you, it's sure to decrease
Children smile, with ease their faces aglow
But as you get older, the smiles sometimes
stop to flow.
Don't block it, don't stop it for goodness sake
Give a big smile and then one do take.

12.

Pick yourself up off that floor.
And start to do something more.
Chaos havoc everywhere,
Yet no one seems to dare.
The system that is destroying
our children's future,
I hear them crying.
Start to listen, start to care
Demand what's right, that seems fair.
If you don't then no one else will, and
guess who's going to foot the bill.

13.

Change starts within, not without
going forward means,
there's no room for doubt.
Ahead lies the answers
that will us release,
from so much disease.
Don't delay now, start to go
so that God's pure energy
can start to flow.
Through your heart and
through your soul.
Saving you once more from
that big black hole.

14.

Forgiving is releasing
Don't you forget.
When someone errs you
with no regret.
Anger and hurt will tie you to pain.
And you'll see there's nothing to gain.
Except in forgiveness,
with no one to blame.

15.

The light of Christ burns so bright
Yet so few of us see.
What is the cause of all this blindness?
Can someone please tell me?
I am frightened, I am scared of all this
darkness about.
Yet I know in my heart without any doubt,
his flame has never gone out.
So please I beg, open your eyes
before anyone else dies.
Without knowledge of that light
that is always shining, oh so bright.
For each and every one of us
The Lord, he waits without the
slightest fuss.

16.

Step by step, the nearer they draw
To help and to guide you, don't clutch at straws,
The truth is simple,
The truth is clear,
So why for God's sake is there all this fear?
Trusting in man is 'desolation'
Trusting in God, you will always find a solution.

17.

This way, that way, we're always
being pulled,
by material distraction we seem
to be ruled.
We easily trust mad-made inventions.
Yet goes unnoticed God's creations.
Money is needed, that I agree
but things need perspective.
Don't you see?

18.

When life takes a tumble
Don't waste time and grumble.
Look up to Him and pray,
For strength for you to stay,
on the path to glory.
Hey! Or you will be sorry
For wasting precious moments.
Crying, whinging, moaning,
For all you think you've lost
Believe me, it's a small cost.
For getting what He's planned
Eternal life.
Oh so grand.

19.

Just face this time with fortitude
and strength,
To come this far, you've gone
through great lengths,
You may have lost your way
a bit,
And now no matter what
nothing will fit,
Don't be afraid, don't give in,
For the best part yet, is only
hidden
Soon all will be shown
to you in light.
And everything will be alright.

20.

The kindness you have in your heart
Is more than enough to make a start
Lying your way, out of each hiccup won't do
You must stop and make amends too.
Give away, the false reasons
Give away, all the lies
And make a fresh start
Please at least try.

21.

Our children are losing due to our indifference.
Wake up stop snoozing give them some reference.
How will they know which way to go,
If we ourselves have not a clue?
Take time out and be
An adult that can see.
Without a hand to guide,
A child will soon slide into the pain of ignorance.
For if we don't show them, what's right or what's wrong,
They're not to blame for coming on strong.
So please for God's sake,
Don't make the mistake of letting him go wild.
With the excuse he's only a child.
A lot is at stake,
Take no chances with his fate.
Love them and guide them,
Before is too late.

22.

Jealousy and hate,
Against your fellow mate.
Causes so much pain,
Driving you insane,
Love and trust,
Go hand in hand.
Banish your fears and wipe away the tears,
Of your insecurities and doubt.
Give of yourself, with open heart,
And truly then, your life will start.

23.

A friend is someone
In whom you can trust.
Who will share with you, even his last crust.
Good times and bad times,
Whatever they be.
With a friend beside you,
I think you'll agree.
Life is made easier and soon trouble free.

24.

Loneliness can become hard to bear,
When there's no one to share,
The joy, the suffering of the day
The chitter chatter of what we'd say.
Being alone can be sad,
But now I've found God,
I am so glad,
He is my friend,
He is my joy,
No more alone am I.

25.

Creating your own chances,
Most certainly enhances.
The quality of your life
Letting go of strife.
Changing darkness to light.
Bringing you more
Of all that's in store,
For your happiness.
So go out and do,
Whatever you have to.
For it is the only way
That you will have your day.

26.

Anger is destructive
Forgiveness is constructive.
Allow yourself to be
A creative energy.
Be a light being
And become all seeing.
Never faltering, never fumbling.
Standing tall, never tumbling.
Learning then teaching,
But never, ever preaching.
For much will be learnt
From the example you set.
Be kind and tolerant
Forgive and forget.

27.

Your life is but a moment,
on this precious earth.
Make the most of every second
right from the time of birth.
Don't waste time dreaming
of things you have not.
Or you surely lose the things you have got!
So get on and enjoy the good times.
And learn your lessons from the bad times.

28.

When you are alone and have
nothing to do.
And it's often times when you're feeling blue.
Allow yourself to drift into God's space.
Where a beautiful picture you
will begin to trace.
With your mind's eye
you can see yourself fly.
Let go of all your fears,
wipe away your tears
and dream a little.

29.

God's law is simple
His love is too.
Why then are we so mixed up?
Pray! Tell me do.
The problems all around us
were surely not His creed
We war on one another
Deprive each other's needs.
We cause the imbalance
of that there is no doubt.
Yet we point a finger at Him
Asking him what's it all about.

30.

Our fellow man is suffering can't you see?
Or are you too afraid to hear his misery?
When will you stop and listen to his cries?
Or are you going to wait, and
watch as another soul dies?
We owe it to ourselves, to make some amends,
to fight for their rights
until authority sends.
All that they need, and make sure they are freed,
from another man's destruction
and misuse of power.
So please – don't let's wait
until the last hour.

31.

The answers you seek
are in safe keep;
buried oh! So deep.
In your subconscious mind.
Seeming at times, so hard to find.
But when you find the key
you will surely see.
How very simple, it really can be.
Knock on the gates of Heaven,
and watch them open wide.
Take a peek within and see
God's paradise.
So beautiful, so glorious,
So wonderfully grand.
All the answers you will find
in God's Holy Land.

32.

Gossip and slander is the devil's tool.
He uses it wisely, mostly to rule.
The petty and ignorant,
he sets up with ease.
Their tongues wagging dangerously
wicked words they release.
Your dishonour is their intent,
causing disruption and pain
is their enjoyment.
So give them no fuel, for their fire
And don't fall and be the devil's liar.
Oh so grand.

33.

Stop and listen to the silence
The answers to all is in abundance
Sweet is the sound of harmony
missed sadly by so many
Soft are the voices saying
come to the master praying
His touch is so gentle
His voice is so kind
In his soft embrace
you are sure to find
All that you lack
open your eyes
Your self-esteem is back.

34.

Make a clean break
There's too much at stake
Allow nothing to hold
Be strong, be bold
Now is the time
It's your turn to shine
Forget doubt of failing
From now on it's plain sailing
You've got what is takes
So for heaven's sake
Make sure you use it
Before you lose it.

35.

Whenever you're in doubt
Be sure to take time out
For mistakes can sometimes cost
And chances can be lost
A few moments longer
Are sure to make you stronger
Bringing sanity and sense
To something that was dense.

36.

The pain you endure
Stressful times you're insecure
Be strong, don't give in
Allow yourself some time for 'livin''.
Banging your head
Against a brick wall,
Won't do much good at all.
Just slow down, relax
That's the key.
Soon you'll be trouble free.

37.

Be a little angel,
Send a little love out,
Spare a thought for others,
A helping hand hold out,
Make a small sacrifice,
And try for that day, to be nice.
For if we all, for a moment gave instead of took,
Our lives, would be richer and would have a
Brighter look.
So my friend do heed this and learn to give,
Only then will life hold any meaning,
And be a joy to live.

38.

The burden can sometimes
be hard to bear,
Learning life's lessons can
sometimes cause doubt and despair.
But there's always a reason
and cause.
He's trying to show you a simple
way, so pause.
Once you understand the reason
behind your pain
You'll see it's not all been in vain.

39.

Get rid of ego,
anger and hate
Make amends with yourself
before it's too late
The self-inflated 'I'
must be allowed to die
for there's no room to grow
If you continue to crow
about all of who you are
And all that you can do
Acting like a star
There's others out there too
so make room to share
and really show you care
less words more action
and you'll be the star attraction!

40.

The painful path or easy way out,
Which one is it going to be?
The one that teaches you to see
as well as sets you free?
Or the one that leads nowhere
with nothing or no one to share?
So think before you take a step
for the answer is right there.

41.

Sometimes we may need a little shove
To take notice of Him above
Feeling neglected? Feeling blue?
I think God has feelings too.
So don't you forget Him never
For He's your friend forever
Allow Him some time, allow Him some space
Show Him how much we need His grace
Ask Him kindly for a warm embrace.

42.

Tomorrow is another day
Just you wait and see
Don't lose faith come what may
And do listen to me,
Though times may test
And you may need a rest
Let nothing come between you
and your destiny,
For troubles and sorrows
Show you the way
Even though they cause you dismay,
Just take heart and know
For every seed you sow
A beautiful tree will grow.

43.

Looking back, I am there now
Seeing your face, remembering how
We were as one, you and I
Never imagining our love could ever die.
Going forward seems so very hard
Without you, I am always on guard
Feeling hurt, feeling blue
Makes no difference what I do.
Why did you have to go away?
I wish there was something that
I could say
To change your mind about how you feel
To show you that I love you a great deal
To prove my love give me a chance
Together once more a dream romance.

44.

What is love?
I ask myself,
And strangely I do not know
Experiencing life's emotions the highs the lows
It seems quite apparent, that love is the cause
of most our woes.
In each of us, it manages to bring out
The beauty, and the beast
The latter not so pleasant to say the least.
The only love I understand,
Is the unconditional kind
Truer than mother's love will be hard to find
But the rest remains a mystery
How does something so special
Cause such misery?

45.

Remove the veil of guilt
The veil of doubt
Listen! Hear my silent shout
I want you to know
Soon very soon the clouds will part
Letting sunshine in
Allowing life to restart.
So lift your spirits high in the air
Join your hands together in prayer
Don't allow the troubles that are
Here to test.
Distract you from the truth
And from doing your best.

46.

There will be times, when life seems
difficult and unfair.
Prayers unanswered, a lonely stare.
When sadness enfolds every layer
of your heart and your soul.
You must never lose sight of your goal.
Like a child you must trust,
unconditionally giving whatever is needed
The now is important and that should be
heeded,
Don't look into the future, don't turn around
or you may just miss what it is you have found
By touch or with words the chance to feel
Allow yourself God's power to heal.

47.

There is so much turmoil around
Problems need solving
Answers to be found
Dear friend, I ask you
Take a moment or two
To contribute whatever you can
Helping your fellow man
Fighting ignorance and injustice
Must be our greatest task you see
For there is no other way
We can all stay
On this beautiful planet
We call Earth
It is now time for our rebirth.

48.

When you have to start all over again
And your previous efforts have all been in vain
Don't think twice of having another go
For this time your true self might glow
The trials and tests
That you've been through
Had a reason and purpose, of that you
Can be sure
So go take another chance
And have yourself a merry little dance.

49.

Christmas is here, once more
Santa will soon be knocking on your door
Bringing with him, gifts galore
Lots of surprises for you in store
But don't you forget, the less fortunate ones
Spare a thought give a chance
To someone who has no one
Toys, food or just bare necessities
Give a little they depend on you generosity
The problems around are so many
But maybe for just one day
Things could look bright and sunny.

50.

The dreams you dream
The thoughts you think
Can lift your spirits up
Unless you let it sink
So take note of all that's in your mind
And use only thoughts of the positive kind
The negative is there to trip you up
In your mind present sure to corrupt
If you are weak, you will surely fall
But if you are strong, you will stand tall
Make the most of all your positive qualities
And all dreams can be realities.

51.

When you are at a point of disillusion
And you lack the ability to see
When your spirit is trapped and longs
To be set free
When the simplest of tasks becomes a mountain to climb.
And your thoughts are only of the negative kind
Where do you go, what do you do?
Do you run around in circles?
Point your finger to
Blame another person, or God himself
up there?
Do you cry a lot, about life not being fair?
Stop, I tell you my dear friend
I have been there too
And found if I stopped blaming and
looked within in truth
The answers came slowly
And I was saved surely.

52.

Money problems can wear you down
Life gets difficult, you wear a frown
How do you overcome problems
of the material kind?
How do you let spiritual thoughts
in when you've been made so blind?
By the grip of negativity you are held
Your future from you seems withheld
By my own experience, please take hope
And don't struggle on trying to cope
On your own you think you are
and your goal seems so very far
First in yourself you must believe
Then in the helper, who has been sent
to relieve
The symptoms of being without
Just trust a little and don't doubt.

53.

Are you happy? Or are you sad?
Does life make you grumble or
make you glad?
Are you a giver, or do you take?
Do you keep silent, just for peace's sake?
It's time to take stock
It's time you unlocked
The real you within
And all your talents, so far hidden
For be sure to know
For every sure step you take
There's going to be a lucky break.

54.

When with child and in need,
People do exploit you
Your feelings, your space
Your need to express
Is totally ignored to this
I can confess.
The things you must go through
The hard times you must face
For survival's sake, your pride
has no place.
For love you search, or maybe
a friend to hold
Mostly they leave you in the cold,
The thing to remember and hold on to
Is that you are special, and that there is
someone who will love you,
Don't let the thoughtless ones
Rule your destiny
Be brave, stand tall and be who you
want to be.

55.

When the one you love, has let you down
And life has no special meaning
When all that once was is no more
It is so hard, it is so sad
At times like these you feel quite bad
Care do I take, not to slide
Into the trap of self-pity, you must ride
Out this time with strength and confidence
Something new will soon commence
Just allow yourself some time to heal
When the time is right you will be able to feel
A new and stronger you
And for sure you will get all you are due.

56.

Don't doubt the power of God
Don't fear because you suffer pain
Once you understand you will gain
So give up, let go of all that is vain
Through experience only you can learn
Books and teachers can do so much
The rest you have to earn
So see what life is teaching you
Make note of where you are heading to
Don't get complacent, don't get blue
Always try and keep your heart simple
and true
and there won't be anything you cannot do.

57.

Kindness of heart, goodness of soul
Is the essence of what we should be
Without a doubt with the gentle touch
You can achieve so much
If we keep our thoughts simple and pure
There may be a chance we could cure
So many of our troubles and woes
Making things friendlier not so many foes
For if we strive for inner peace
Going forward would be with the
greatest of ease.

58.

The chances we get
We lose when we fret
For nothing is gained
When life's hurts, leave us pained
In order to succeed
We must first be freed
From all that is causing us upset
From all that is causing unrest
Until that is done
Life will be no fun.

59.

Imagine a life without the sun,
wind and rain
Imagine a life that only knows
pain.
Imagine a life where there's no
glimmer of hope.
Imagine a life, that just can't cope.
So many out there are just that way
Given up, gone astray.
Misguided and misunderstood
These poor souls need help
For sure you could.
Make them start to see and feel
again.
Your love and effort will heal them
again.

60.

Words if spoken correctly can
undo so many wrongs.
If put to music could be sung
as songs.
Together joined to make
poetry and rhymes.
Words can be written to express
past and present times.
By the written word so much
we now know.
By our spoken word new seeds
we can sow.
So make sure you use your
words with pride and sense.
And brighten up, all that is
still dense.

61.

Thoughts; we all the time do think.
Thoughts flying around too many
to link.
We don't need to think so much
but we do.
If only we could stop for a moment or two.
The voice in the silence would be clear to you.
The problems you have it would
guide you through.
It cannot be heard unless you are
still.
So stop for a moment and let it your
heart fill.

62.

When will man learn
to love, not burn?
The senselessness of yesterday,
There surely must be another way
Violence on one hand,
The other side greed.
Hatred and anger,
on each other's weaknesses we feed.
In the name of peace, so many are
slain,
Precious life is lost,
so little is gained.
There is more than enough to go
around,
If only a little compassion is found.
A little more goodwill and trust,
in each other to find is a must
Or else this life we live in vain
No progress forward only more pain.

63.

God is patient
So must you be
If you rush, you will not see
All that He is trying to show you.
In time; giving you what's due
Don't despair, don't give in
Have patience and you will win.

64.

Make it happen
Make it right
Just by thinking
Thoughts so bright.
Guide yourself towards
your goal.
Speak within your soul.
You will be shown, so many
things new.
You will develop a broader view
So don't waste any more time
my friend
A treasure within, you will find
Just as God did intend.

65.

Selfish thoughts, selfish ways,
Will get you nowhere, empty days.
Always wanting more than you need,
Will leave you disappointed, coz it's greed.
When 'ego' demands more than it's due,
You'll find your friends are only few.
Spiritually you cannot grow or learn,
If your main concern is how much you'll earn.
It's good to be ambitious and want a little more,
Just as long as you have a kind and gentle core
It's good when life deals you a good hand,
But by sharing your good fortune with others
you'll feel more grand.
So don't get absorbed in wanting and wanting,
Or life may end up being pretty daunting.

66.

Your ego is so demanding
It can lead you astray
It pulls you in all directions
The truth is kept at bay.
Within each of us so hidden
are gems so pure
Only found by us, when some
pain we endure
Each time when some part
of your ego, you let go
You'll find greater understanding
and of yourself, new things you will know.

67.

Thank you, God, for this here life
Thank you, God, for the strength in strife
Thank you for the lessons learnt
Nearly gave up if there you weren't
Still so much to learn and do
I want so much to please you
My life in your service I do give
In righteousness help me live
To spread your healing rays of love
I offer myself to you above.

68.

Towards a better way of life
you must aim
Or everything will always remain
the same
So much is out there for you
to make
So many opportunities you
could take
For you will never know until
you try
To find your hidden talents you
must pry
Persevere and you will find
You can come out from behind.

69.

The voice of temptation is always
calling,
And if you are not careful, you will
start falling,
From God's grace and chosen goal.
Your weaknesses tested,
do try harder to be a model role.
To overcome your flaws,
Courage and discipline you need.
Make a plan, stick to it and you
will succeed.

70.

Don't worry, when a little you slide
Just be sure in God's law you abide
For all that you need will be soon at hand
Providence has made sure, you safely will land
Don't forget to share your good will
And your future will be even
brighter still.

71.

Seek not you, all that is vain.
Seek but you, the answers that remain.
Hidden within the silence of mind,
Words of wisdom, thoughts so kind.
There is much more than you can see,
But first you must be set free.
From all that you doubt
From all that you fear.
Then the truth will be quite clear.

72.

God is within
God is without
So why in God's name
is there all this doubt
You must believe that
you are in his care
Stop all your worrying and to
Him your soul do bare
The minute you trust
Your success depends on
it so you must
Forget past mistakes and be
all that He needs you to be
Lighten up, and let go and
watch your true self flow.

73.

The devil he comes to tempt and tease,
Your life he plays with, with such ease,
You must be strong and not give in,
He has no power, he cannot win.
You foolishly slide into the trap he sets,
When you lose faith, your soul he gets.
Nothing he says or does is real, or true.
So pray to God, for only He loved you.

74.

You have lost so much in search of more
Love and happiness, was once at your door.
Material cares now wear you down
And life leaves you wearing a frown.
You trust what you see, and not what you feel.
Consequences are you got a raw deal.
Your vision is marred by vanity,
Your dreams are now far from reality.

75.

Mistakes made, lessons learnt
The old ways now are dead and burnt
Ahead you must go truth to find
Now that you're no longer blind
Once more you must put your
Trust and faith in God unseen
For you know on Him you can lean
You have failed Him for the last time ever
From now on its Him forever.

76.

Living life in delusion
causes so much pain.
Slowly but surely, it will
drive you insane.
You must wake up and see,
where you are going wrong.
Search your weaknesses or
before long,
They will catch you out and
trip you up.
And you will be left holding an
empty cup.
Meet your fears face to face
Defy the odds and you'll
win the race.

77.

The trials and tests you endure
Are of small significance of that
you can be sure.
For the gift of understanding and
being able to truly see
is the greatest gift God has given
us, hidden beneath misery.
For when you understand the
lesson behind your pain
You will see it's not been in vain
And learning the truth is man's
highest gain.

78.

Just as love can nurture and
help you grow
It can also destroy and harden your core
Too much can smother
Too little can pain
Get a balance, or go insane.
To each of us, to use or abuse in this
life we live
We cannot change anyone only the 'I'
So begin by letting all the negative die
For if in your heart is bitterness and pain
From falling in love, please do refrain.

79.

Believe in yourself, just have a little faith
Having faith yourself is a must
for what else is left, if in yourself you
don't trust?
What you are about to do right
and your goal should soon be in sight
But if you don't take the first step
Then from your destiny you will be kept.

80.

God He is our maker, there above
all He has ever given us is love
He awaits us, with arms open wide
Beautiful angels he has on either side
He calls out to us, soft and gentle
when we stray
Whispering, come to me child, kneel
and pray
Even when we don't heed His voice
giving into temptation, making the wrong choice
Patiently and with love He helps you see
Though you strayed from his side
never did He
So no matter how bad things get
Just look up to Him don't fret
He will listen, He will heal
With him you always get a better deal

81.

A new day dawns, yet nothing much has changed,
We have come this far, but things still need to be
rearranged.
Technology is fast moving.
Scientists, new theories are always proving.
Outer space has been reached,
God's law is being preached,
Yet nothing has changed.
Spiritually we lack, most of us do not see,
We are tied to our ignorance, from which we need
to be freed.
Only when we learn to love one another,
Sharing what we have, helping our sisters and
brothers.
Only when we can see, with love in our eyes,
Forgiving one another, telling no more lies,
Will there be any real change, in the progress of
man.
So sit up take notice and change what you can.

82.

Keeping bad company will lead you astray.
They have no direction, and should be
kept at bay.
They use and abuse, whatever they can.
They have no respect for their fellow man.
Don't be weak and follow their ways.
Stay true to yourself for that's what pays.
By being strong, a fine example you will set.
And for sure God's blessing you will get.

83.

Sometimes when life is upside down
and you don't know what to do
Sit down and be still, and listen to
what I am telling you.
You do need to stop
You do need to care
or you will continue to wear
yourself into the ground
where no answers can be found.
Caring for others is noble indeed
But first your own needs you must heed
For if you don't stop and have a rest
Realising your goals will be a great test.

84.

Why do some lie?
Why do some cheat?
Why do some, loved ones beat?
Why do some go crazy and kill?
Why do some incestuously abuse?
Answers nil!
The victims of these awful acts
Suffer endlessly and those are facts
Don't they have a conscience?
Don't they see?
Pray someone do tell me!

85.

At some point in life
We do ask 'why?'
To Him up there in the sky
When life suddenly trips us up
And we are holding an empty cup
To God we do seem to turn
When some disaster we do earn
God did not create the mess we're in
Yet, he forgives us, when again we sin
For what counts to Him is our soul
To reach it to Heaven is his goal
So what happens to this outer
shell we live in
Is the price for going to Heaven
For lessons are only learnt
through pain
We cannot see his plan yet for we are
still selfish and vain.

86.

Without prayer, with God you have no link
Spare a moment and of Him do think,
Don't only look to Him in time of need,
or when from some problem you need
to be freed
Speak to Him every day without fail,
and you will find through life you will sail
A word of thanks or a word of glee
look up to God and the devil will flee
You cannot fail, if in your thoughts
you have Him
Go on open your heart and let Him in.

87.

Start to paint a picture
within your mind
Colour it brightly with thoughts
so kind
Liven it up with humour so bold
Make sure the sun's shining a
beautiful gold
Frame it all round with memories
that make you smile
Stop and look at this masterpiece
for a while
Now sign it with love in your name
And treasure it always
there's no two the same.

88.

There is more to life than meets the eye,
There is more to death than the tears we cry
Why are we here? Why do we leave?
Pain and suffering, we all do grieve.
Yet on one another we war.
Precious life is taken in the name of the law
If peace is what is being sought,
How come more arms are being bought.
You cannot fight fire with fire I'm told,
So why are they doing just that?
Oh! I'm cold
It seems the only way, we now know, how to
speak and be heard,
Is by holding a gun to someone's head.
It's getting absurd.
The people in power are surely to blame
If they got things right, there would not
Be this shame.
All you parents and teachers, it starts with you
Governing bodies, prime ministers and presidents too
Religious leaders, you especially, a stand must take
Stop fighting one another, for heaven's sake
Our children are our only hope,
On their own they cannot cope.
If they are not taught lessons from our foolish
Mistakes and negative attitudes,
Another generation will grow to feud.
The vicious circle will just go on,
Until one day, we all will be gone.

89.

Someone somewhere needs you,
Loneliness, leaves you lost and cold
When memories are your only company
and worth their weight in gold.
But is that enough? Is that fair?
Looking back, combing your grey hair
We all need someone
A friend to share
the empty hours, the highs and lows
This problem needs solving this I do know
Maybe if we all tried a little more
To give some time to comfort and
befriend someone who is low
Richer our lives would be made
and another's loneliness would soon fade.

90.

Dance with God any time you feel down
Dance with God when you wear a frown
Lose yourself in his perfect rhythm of love
When your spirit is broken he handles you
with kid gloves
And if you feel like a bit of rock & roll
God will oblige, for he loves your soul.

91.

A garden of beauty is a pleasure to see
Full of spring colours and sounds of glee
The birds in the trees,
The bees buzzing round,
The scent of roses
Your senses astound
The cool breeze blows gently
The rustling through grass and leaves
The invisible source of life through
everything does weave
Yet all these miracles slip us by without
second thought
We still foolishly question Gods presence
When we are fraught.

92.

When you don't understand
and feel under strain
When all your efforts have gone
down the drain
When all your prayers, and all
your pleads
Get you nowhere, and your heart
does bleed.
When at this point you find
yourself stuck
And you seem to be all out of luck
Take a deep breath, let go of it all
For in the eternal plan, your problems
are so small.
Just know, when the time comes,
God will answer your call
So don't allow yourself anymore to fall.

93.

Every cloud has a silver lining
or so I've heard them say
Just hold on to your dreams
No matter how much the dismay
The price you have to pay
for your dreams to come true
Can sometimes leave you feeling
totally unglued
Your hard work and effort can
sometimes go unnoticed
But you must remember always
to keep yourself focused
on all that you want and all that
you need.
Making sure always there is no
room for greed.

94.

Welcome into your heart,
the spirit of love.
Being sent to you warmly,
from Him above,
For you need his healing
rays of light,
Shining down brightly even
in the dead of night.
Just allow yourself to be
given this gift.
From the depths of sadness you
it will surely lift.
You cannot go forward from
where you're at,
Don't worry soon it will be your
turn to bat.

95.

Let the little things in life
make you glad
When you're feeling unhappy
and feeling rather sad.
There's a hundred unnoticed
blessings all around your
saddened heart.
They will help heal your pain,
so why don't you start!
To count all your blessings,
one by one.
For a start, look up at the sun.

96.

When you live in selfishness and greed
You block out light, that you so need
Closed to all else, you see only you,
You forget others and what they are due
You cannot go on this way my friend
For sure you will find it's a dead end
Try and give a little back each day
And you will see, how much it will pay.

97.

Set yourself a target,
and see what you can do
Push yourself harder and find
the real you
You can accomplish anything
if only you would try,
Sitting and waiting,
for wasted years, you will cry,
Life is too short, so don't you wait
Get off your backside,
Before it's too late.

98.

Even though you may be tired,
Even though you may be worn,
Even though your dreams have
been broken,
Even though your heart's been
torn.
Know that precious life is worth
living and new dreams can be
found.
After every dark night, a bright
new day begins.
This is as sure as the world goes
round.
Just have faith, work a little harder
and good things will come your way.

99.

Feel free to be happy,
Feel free to enjoy,
All that life is offering,
Ignore all that does annoy,
Use the next few moments
for your own pleasure,
Make a few happy memories,
in your heart to treasure,
Sometimes its OK to be selfish
Just for a while.
Especially when people around you,
are cramping up your style.

100.

The human shell we live in,
Is only a disposable case.
Inside is living a special being,
that needs, your warm embrace.
The body is important of that there is
no doubt.
But your spirit too needs nourishing,
for so long it goes without.
By your experiences, and
understanding
It gets stronger each day.
And shines even brighter when you
call out and pray.
You soul is 'eternal' of that you
should know.
So tend to it each moment and watch
how in strength it will grow.